Join my facebook coloring group and get a lot of free coloring books and coloring pages

IMPRESSUM
Monsoon Publishing LLC:
Info@monsoonpublishing.de
www.monsoonpublishing.de
facebook.com/monsoonpublishingllc

IMPRESS
Monsoon Publishing LLC
nfo@monsoonpublishing.com
www.monsoonpublishing.com
facebook.com/monsoonpublishingusa
group: monsoon publishing coloring group

Printed in the USA
CPSIA information can be obtained
at www.ICGtesting.com
LVHW081256210924
791651LV00011B/291

9 783758 498022